KITCHEN WELLNESS

Beauty from the Inside-Out

Krystal Champion

Balboa Press books may be ordered through booksellers or by contacting:

Balboa Press
A Division of Hay House
1663 Liberty Drive
Bloomington, IN 47403
www.balboapress.com
1 (877) 407-4847

ISBN: 978-1-9822-0463-1 (sc)
ISBN: 978-1-9822-0462-4 (e)

Library of Congress Control Number: 2018906425

Print information available on the last page.

Balboa Press rev. date: 06/15/2018

BALBOA
PRESS
A DIVISION OF HAY HOUSE

Contents

Dedication..v

Introduction..vii

Simple Guidelines..ix

Stocking Your Kitchen for Wellness...x

Vitamins and Minerals...xiii

Blueberry Banana Oatmeal...1

Honey Blueberry Facial Scrub..2

Acai Protein Bowl...5

Acai Cleansing Mask..6

Green Tea and Cucumber Popsicles..7

Green Tea and Cucumber Ice Facial and Eye Treatment.................8

Collard Green Wrap with Turmeric Sauce.......................................10

Brightening Cleansing Grains..11

Tomato-Basil Cucumber Tart..12

Tomato-Basil Acne Treatment..14

Scallops with Avocado-Grapefruit Salsa...17

Lightening Acne Mask...18

Artichoke with Lemon-Thyme Dipping Oil.......................................20

Lemon, Thyme, and Fennel Cleanser...22

Roasted Beet, Avocado, and Grapefruit Salad...............................23

Soothing Grapefruit and Avocado Face Mask.................................24

Kale Salad with Poached Egg..26

Kale Firming Mask and Eye Treatment...27

Tangy Carrot Salad...28

Carrot and Goji Facial Cleanser..31

Raw Superfood Balls...32

Vitality Facial Scrub..33

Invigorating Peppermint-Orange Tea..34

Youthful Eye Treatment...35

Forbidden Black Rice with Shrimp..36

Black Rice and Ginger-Coconut Scrub..38

Gluten Free Coffee-Carob Chip Biscotti...40

Energizing Coffee Scrub..43

Avocado-Papaya Salad..44

Avocado-Papaya Face and Body Mask..46

Pumpkin-Sage Quinoa..48

Anti-Aging Pumpkin Clay Skin Healer..51

Pure Bliss Herbal Tea...52

Herbal Relaxing Bath Soak...54

Watermelon Salad 56
Watermelon-Hydrating Skin Healer 57
Roasted Veggies with Cayenne Pepper... 58
Cayenne Pepper Pain-Relief Cream 60
Turmeric-Ginger Dip... 62
Turmeric and Ginger Stretch Mark Oil 64
Avocado-Cacao Pudding.. 67
Hydrating Avocado-Cacao Body Mask 68
Monster Green Smoothie 70
Detoxifying Spirulina Face and Body Mask 72
Power Granola Bars 75
After-Sun Skin Healer... 76
Cucumber-Melon Mojito.. 79
Mojito Foot Soak and Scrub... 80
Grilled Peaches with Rosemary and Balsamic Reduction...................................... 82
Rosemary Oil Hair Treatment.. 84
Carrot-Ginger Soup with Goji Berries 86
Carrot-Coconut Moisture Hand Mask.. 88
Blooming Red Onion Flower 90
Strengthening Onion Hair Treatment.. 92
Health Nut Banana Muffins... 93
Moisturizing Hair Mask 94
Lemony Rainbow Cabbage Salad... 96
Lemon Nail Strengthener and Brightener 98
Beet Detox Juice.. 99
Beet Lip Stain.. 100

Dedication

To my amazing family, who have always been by my side, providing me with the foundation of what is real and showing me how to love. True beauty lies within, at the core of our existence. A special shout-out to my talented sister Kym for her brilliant photos.

To my husband and my beautiful children, who have taught me what really matters in life. A humbling experience that has taught me to be present in every moment, enjoy the simple things in life, and to love with all my heart. You are my inspiration, my heart, and my soul. I love you with every ounce of my being.

To my dear friends: thank you for offering your inspiration and helping me to see my vision, bringing it to a reality. A special thank-you to Lisa Michaelis for inspiring and pushing me to make this book.

And finally, I wish to offer a special dedication to you for pursuing your quest for wellness. You have begun a journey I hope brings you unlimited joy, health, and light.

Introduction

What you eat, what you put on your body, and how you treat the world have a dramatic impact on the way you look and feel. Your kitchen holds the secret to looking and feeling vibrant. I created this cookbook as a fun and easy guide that reveals how to achieve beauty from the inside out by using items from your kitchen. As a busy working mom, I never really had time to enjoy spa treatments, even though I've been in the health and beauty industry for over eighteen years and know the importance of taking care of oneself. I crafted this book with the goal to help others enjoy delicious, healthy recipes that can double as at-home spa treatments without all the nasty additives in even the most expensive food and beauty products. The result? Here's an easy way to look and feel your best—naturally. Throughout this book, you will find recipes that will guide you on your path to a more holistic lifestyle, feed the body, and soothe the soul.

Throughout history, in both Eastern and Western cultures, healers have recognized the importance of what we put in our bodies. Healthy skin, hair, and nails can be achieved only if your body is healthy and functioning properly. When you have deficiencies in your diet, you will start to see signs of thinning hair, brittle nails, acneic skin, and many other disorders. Beauty starts from the inside. It's important to maintain a well-balanced diet that nourishes the body. When you feel good, you look good and radiate a glow that brightens the world.

It might sound silly, but your kitchen holds a great deal of beauty essentials, and I promise you will find it fun to experiment and concoct at-home spa products. A few years back, after having my daughter, I dramatically changed my diet to focus on healthy, plant-based food and eliminated a great deal of meat, dairy, and sugar. I started feeling better, and my skin and hair staring looking better. I then started to realize that what I was putting *on* my body was just as important as what I was putting *into* it. I began to look at labels. As someone who has purchased thousands of beauty products for both personal and professional use, I started to find that even the products I thought were "safe" and "natural" had horrible ingredients that have been shown to be toxic.

Your skin is the largest and fastest growing organ of the body. What we put on our skin is just as important as what we put in our bodies. Less than 2 percent of what you ingest gets to your skin to nourish it, so it is extremely important to ensure you add some rituals into your regimen to achieve a glowing, radiant appearance. What you put on your skin topically can dramatically affect your health as well. Many of the over-the-counter lotions, serums, and beauty product contain harsh chemicals that are toxic. It takes less than one minute for some products applied to the hair and skin to get into the bloodstream. With the average person applying over ten different products daily to his or her hair, body, and skin, that's thousands of chemicals going right into your body, causing toxic buildup. So the question is, What are you applying to your body, and is it safe? Every recipe in *Kitchen Wellness* has been carefully created to ensure it is chemical free, organic, and safe.

If we don't eat foods offering the nutrients we need, our bodies can't produce hormones correctly or maintain hormonal balance because they don't have the proper building blocks to do so. Our hormones control our mood, digestion, energy—and yes, even how our skin and hair look and feel. Basing your meals on clean proteins, hormone-balancing healthy fats, antioxidant-rich veggies, and healing herbs will help your body maximize its highest potential.

You may have heard the buzzword *superfood*. While all plant food offers a multitude of nutritional benefits, there are a handful of foods that contain exceptionally dense nutrient concentrations. These are known as superfoods and grow in specific regions all over the world. By adding just one superfood per day to your diet, you can drastically change your health, radiance, and overall well-being.

I'm often stopped and asked what I use on my skin. I'm honored to share my secrets, and I tell people this: "It's simple. We are what we eat. When you begin to eat for beauty, you become beautiful. You become mindful and present. It changes the way you approach things in your everyday life. Your kitchen holds all the beauty secrets you need for beauty and longevity." Beauty truly starts from the inside, and we can help it along with the healing foods we eat and apply to our bodies. This is an inside-out approach to make you look and feel radiant.

Simple Guidelines

Although we are using fresh, organic, and healthy ingredients, it's important to understand that every body is different, and some people may have different reactions to ingredients. Please follow the suggestions below to ensure proper use of the ingredients and recipes in this book.

Using fresh ingredients, such as herbs, fruits, and vegetables, enables you to capture the benefits at their peak. When using ingredients topically, it's important to understand that fresh ingredients have a short shelf life, and it's suggested that you use them right away or store them in an airtight container in the refrigerator for no longer than five days, unless otherwise denoted.

When applying the at-home spa recipes, I suggest that you do a patch test to ensure there are no reactions to the ingredients used.

If you are allergic to any of the ingredients used in the recipes, please omit that ingredient or substitute something else.

Because we are using natural, organic ingredients, the results for some of the recipes may take longer, but the benefits will become apparent with repeated use. You will look and feel great, knowing you are doing amazing things for yourself.

It's always suggested that you speak with a medical professional before starting any type of new diet or beauty routine. If you have any concerns or reactions from any of the recipes, please stop using them and contact your medical professional immediately.

Stocking Your Kitchen for Wellness

Setting yourself up for success is key to achieving and maintaining wellness, which is why I suggest stocking your kitchen with these essentials to help you achieve your goals along your wellness journey. When you eliminate the temptation to eat unhealthy snacks and food within your environment, you create good habits of eating whole foods designed by nature to bring you wellness and abundance.

Acai

Native to the Amazon rainforest, ancient tribes have used acai for thousands of years as food and medicine. One of nature's most concentrated source of antioxidants, acai is an amazing superfood.

Apple Cider Vinegar

Apple cider vinegar is a wonderful digestive tonic that prevents constipation, boosts energy, and helps to fight bad bacteria. Apple cider vinegar helps to balance acidic foods in the body to maintain a healthy pH. Great for the kitchen to flavor foods and exceptional in home spa remedies, apple cider vinegar is an absolute must-have.

Cacao

Dating back to ancient Mayan times, cacao is the raw and natural form of chocolate. In its most unprocessed state, it is one of the most antioxidant-rich foods on the planet. Cacao doesn't just taste good; it makes you feel good.

Coconut Oil

An absolute staple, coconut oil has so many purposes. It is made of anti-inflammatory, medium-chain fatty acids, which burn quickly and easily in the body without being broken down by the liver, allowing for instant energy. Coconut oil actually helps to boost metabolism. I keep it not only in my pantry but also in my bathroom for use as a moisturizer, toothpaste, oil pulling, and much more.

Coconut Sugar

A great alternative to white or brown sugar, coconut sugar is rich in vitamins and minerals, and it has about half the glycemic index of cane sugar.

Coconut Water

A staple in our house for me and my kids, coconut water is packed with natural hydration and electrolytes. Staying hydrated is extremely important for the body to function properly. Coconut water, made from young Thai coconuts, has been dubbed "Mother Nature's sports drink" and can help replace lost hydration and electrolytes. Just make sure you purchase the natural version with no added sugar.

Chia Seeds

A staple food among the Mayans, Incas, and Aztecs, chia has been known to provide the body with a multitude of benefits, including immune system support, cardiovascular health, and reducing inflammation. A complete protein, chia seeds are rich in calcium and zinc, and they are packed with soluble fiber, which improves elimination and reduces bloating. Introducing chia into your diet will help improve your hair, nails, and skin.

Dates

Known as "nature's candy," dates provide instant energy and a great deal of nutrients, such as potassium, iron, dietary fiber, and B vitamins. They are a great natural sweetener for desserts, energy balls, or smoothies.

Flaxseed

Similar to chia, flaxseed has a great deal of essential fatty acids, is high in protein, and helps balance hormone levels. Some studies show flaxseed can help prevent breast cancer thanks to their ability to mimic estrogen in the body. It's best to grind flaxseed prior to use so the body can properly digest it.

Goji Berry

Used in Chinese medicine dating back thousands of years, the goji berry is said to be the secret of longevity. Sometimes called the "longevity fruit," goji berries are some of the most powerful superfoods. They contain over twenty vitamins and minerals, and eighteen amino acids; they are bursting with antioxidants. Goji berries have the exceptional ability to defend mitochondrial health and protect against DNA damage. Goji berries are high in sugar, so use only a small amount.

Maca

Maca root has been used medicinally for thousands of years. Ancient Incan warriors used maca to increase strength and stamina during battles. Maca is loaded with around sixty different phytonutrients, which help to strengthen and balance the body's system to combat fatigue, deal with stressors, and provide long-lasting energy.

Quinoa

Native to South America, quinoa packs a great protein punch and provides a wide variety of vitamins and minerals to help fuel the body and revitalize hair and skin. Quinoa is a great staple for sides or stand-alone salads. It helps support healthy digestion with fiber, balancing the healthy bacteria in the gut.

Sea Buckthorn Oil

A small orange berry that has been used dating back to the Tang Dynasty, sea buckthorn oil is a natural anti-aging agent that is known to help fight inflammation internally. It has remarkable healing properties for skin and hair. Rich in vitamin C and omegas, sea buckthorn oil is a superhero.

Sea Salt

Containing a wide range of trace minerals, such as calcium, iodine, potassium, and magnesium, sea salt helps to flavor food with a healthy purpose. It is exceptional for the skin and helps detoxify the body.

Spirulina

Dating back millions of year, spirulina is an algae that contains a broad range of vitamins and minerals. A powerhouse of proteins, spirulina helps reduce fatigue, detoxifies the body, and improves mental function. It has been used in many cultures to help rebuild nerve tissue, improve the immune system, and fight against cancer.

The food you eat can be either the safest and most powerful
form of medicine or the slowest form of poison.
—Ann Wigmore

I've always had a passion for food, beauty, and well-being. I will admit that I do have indulgences and have eaten my fair share of those delicious chocolate cookies with the suspicious cream inside or the cheesy puffs that leave my fingers orange. Up until I got pregnant with my son, I ate whatever I wanted and didn't really think about how the food I ate impacted my body. Once I was pregnant, I realized I needed to eat cleaner and make better food choices. I began to drink more water, enjoy more fruits and veggies, and cut out certain foods that didn't serve a purpose.

When my father was diagnosed with lung cancer, my world was shattered. My family and I began to research alternatives for his chemotherapy and radiation, in hopes that we could change his mind to eat a special diet, with nutrient-dense foods to battle his cancer. Along the way of my research, I realized how important it is to ensure that you give your body the proper fuel for it to function. I was amazed by reading that certain concoctions of simple kitchen ingredients had halted cancer and assisted in healing other ailments for so many people if they stayed on a specific diet and course for wellness. In my countless hours of research, I found how vitamins and minerals impact the body. Below is a guide to help you understand what these fabulous nutrients within this cookbook can do for the body and how they promote beauty, anti-aging, and overall wellness.

Vitamins and Minerals

Vitamin or Nutrient	Food Source	Benefits
Vitamin A	Carrots, collard greens, kale, pumpkin, spinach, sweet potatoes, papaya	Boosts the immune system, fights cell damage and aids in cellular turnover.
Vitamin B1/Thiamine	Black beans, edamame, eggs, nuts and seeds	Maintains proper heart and nerve function and is vital for energy production.
Vitamin B2/Riboflavin	Spinach, mushrooms, sesame seeds, beet greens	Maintains collagen levels for healthy hair and skin, helps build red blood cells.
Vitamin B3/Niacin	Mushrooms, sunflower seeds, tahini, bell peppers	Calms skin, repairs DNA and improves cholesterol levels.
Vitamin B5/Pantothenic Acid	Avocado, mushrooms, sweet potatoes, bell peppers, cucumbers	Relieves anxiety and stress, helps strengthens hair and nails.
Vitamin B6/Pyridoxine	Garlic, bananas, spinach, avocados, carrots, cabbage	Supports brain function and mood, maintains healthy hair and skin.
Vitamin B7/Biotin	Swiss chard, carrots, cucumbers, raspberries, onions, watermelon, grapefruit	Essential for healthy skin, nails and hair. Improves metabolism.
Vitamin B9/Folate	Sprouts, leafy greens, flaxseed, beets, grapefruit, papaya	Essential for a healthy pregnancy. Helps prevent premature aging.
Vitamin B12	Spirulina, nutritional yeast, scallops, yogurt, shrimp	Helps maintain energy levels, boosts mood and reduces inflammation.

Vitamin C	Kale, papaya, bell peppers, grapefruit, tomatoes	Heals wounds, boosts immune system and collagen, improves texture of skin.
Vitamin D	Mushrooms, eggs, sun	Maintains healthy bones, protects agains ailments and enhances radiance.
Vitamin E	Tomatoes, seeds and nuts, papaya, olive oil, avocados, pumpkin	Blocks free radicals from the body, nourishes skin and hair.
Vitamin K1	Beets, cucumbers, parsley, collard greens, spinach, basil, cayenne pepper	Strengthens blood vessels to help heal bruises and dark circles.
Calcium	Cabbage, kale, chard, pumpkin	Helps regulate hormones, reduce PMS symptoms and is vital for bone health.
Copper	Goji berries, pumpkin and sesame seeds, cashews, coconuts, leafy greens, potatoes, mushrooms, avocados, shrimp	Essential for nerve function. Promotes healthy hair, skin and nails.
CoQ10	Walnuts, sesame seeds and oil, spinach	Protects cells from damage and premature aging. Supports heart and vascular health.
Glutathione	Beets, turmeric, artichokes, cinnamon, grapefruit, watermelon, collard greens, garlic	Boosts the immune system, protects DNA, and regenerates cells.
Iron	Hemp seeds, spirulina, kale, parsley, pumpkin seeds, cacao, oats, shrimp	Strengthens nails and hair, helps transport oxygen throughout the body, and helps fight fatigue. It is essential for overall health.
Magnesium	Coconuts, cashews, quinoa, oatmeal, pumpkin seeds, leafy greens, avocados, bananas, cacao	Helps the body to maintain normal nerve and muscle function, helps combat stress and PMS, and helps to promote healthy bones and teeth.

Manganese	Cinnamon, spinach, oats, flaxseed, cacao, almonds, cashews, green tea	Helps maintain healthy hair, cognitive function and supports bone health.
Omega Fatty Acids (EPA, DHA)	Chia seed, flaxseed and flaxseed oil, hemp seeds, walnuts, spinach, spirulina	This anti-inflammatory regulates mood and hormones, is vital for brain and heart health. Promotes healthy skin and hair.
Phosphorus	Quinoa, pumpkin seeds, scallops, oats, almonds	Repairs DNA, supports a strong immune system, improves digestion and hormonal balance, and strengthens bones and teeth.
Potassium	Bananas, Swiss chard, avocados, mushrooms, dark leafy greens	Helps to maintain the body's pH balance, reduces anxiety and stress, and enhances muscle strength.
Selenium	Coconut water, eggs, mushrooms, oats	Defends against free-radicals, regulates thyroid function and boosts immunity.
Silicon	Cucumbers, cabbage, bananas, oats, apples, grapes, flaxseed	Essential for stronger bones, better looking skin and more flexible joints.
Sodium	Beets, carrots, spinach and Swiss chard, Himalayan salt	Helps to maintain electrolyte balance, helps thyroid function, and reduces stress.
Sulfur	Cacao, arugula, cabbage, kale, garlic, onion	Helps fight acne and skin infections. Aids in the production of collagen.
Zinc	Spinach, mushrooms, cacao, pumpkin seeds, quinoa, sesame seeds, chia seeds, shrimp	Boosts immune system and heals skin. Zinc is vital for cell division and growth.

Blueberry Banana Oatmeal

This energy-boosting breakfast is the perfect way to start the day. Bananas are a great source of potassium, dietary fiber, manganese, and vitamins B6 and C. Blueberries contain antioxidants, which work to neutralize free radicals. Raw honey has antiviral, antibacterial, and antifungal properties. Honey promotes digestive health, is a powerful antioxidant, and strengthens the immune system. An alarming rate of people are vitamin D deficient. Using vitamin D powder will help boost your vitamin D levels to increase energy and mood, and help fight ailments and disease. Vitamin D powder is available at health food stores.

Ingredients

2 medium-sized, ripe, organic bananas, sliced into 1/2-inch pieces

1 1/2 cups organic blueberries, divided

3/4 teaspoon cinnamon, divided

1/4 cup organic raw honey, divided

1 cup uncooked organic quick oats (gluten free)

1/4 cup chopped walnuts, divided organic coconut yogurt

1/2 teaspoon baking powder (aluminum-free)

pinch of salt

3 tablespoons chia seeds

1 cup coconut or almond milk

1 egg

1 teaspoon vanilla extract

vitamin D powder

Preparation

Preheat oven to 375 degrees F. Lightly grease 8-inch-by-8-inch baking dish with coconut oil. Arrange banana slices in a single layer in baking dish. Sprinkle half of blueberries, 1/4 teaspoon cinnamon, and 1 tablespoon honey over the bananas. Bake 15 minutes.

Combine oats, half the nuts, baking powder, salt, remaining cinnamon, and chia seeds. Stir. In a separate bowl, whisk together milk, remaining honey, egg, and vanilla extract.

Remove bananas and blueberries from oven and pour oat mixture over fruit. Pour milk mixture over, making sure to distribute evenly. Sprinkle remaining blueberries and walnuts, then bake for 30 minutes or until golden brown. Serve warm with a spoonful of yogurt and a few dashes of vitamin D powder.

Honey Blueberry Facial Scrub

This gentle yet effective scrub works to increase the radiance and vitality of the skin. Honey is one of nature's greatest skin-care gifts. Not only is it moisturizing, but it also contains antioxidants and has antibacterial properties. Oatmeal acts as a gentle exfoliant, revealing smoother and more youthful skin. It also contains selenium, zinc, and copper to fight wrinkles. Blueberries are naturally rich in vitamin C and contain something called "anthocyanins," which boost collagen levels in the skin. Coconut yogurt is protein rich and full of lauric acid. Coconut yogurt, when applied topically, can tighten the pores. Vitamin D helps to minimize acne, boosts elasticity, stimulates collagen production, enhances radiance, and lessens the appearance of fine lines and dark spots.

Ingredients

1 teaspoon chia seeds

1 1/2 teaspoons coconut water

3–4 tablespoons organic oatmeal

10 organic blueberries

2 tablespoons organic raw honey

1 tablespoon plain coconut yogurt

1 teaspoon vitamin D powder

Preparation

Soak chia seeds in coconut water for 20 minutes. Pulse oatmeal in a food processor or coffee grinder for 10 seconds. Set aside.

Rinse blueberries and place them in a food processor or coffee grinder. Add honey and yogurt, and blend until smooth. Mix in oatmeal and vitamin D powder, and blend for 10 seconds until a smooth paste is formed. Pour into desired container and mix in chia seeds.

Usage

Using fingertips, lightly smooth paste over face and neck in a circular motion, avoiding the eye area. Let set for 10 minutes. Remove with a warm washcloth and splash face with cool water.

Apply your favorite moisturizer onto freshly exfoliated skin to lock in hydration. Discard remaining scrub. You can exfoliate once a week using this nourishing scrub.

Acai Protein Bowl

This heavenly, simple breakfast bowl is full of superfoods and packed with nutrition. Acai is known as a superfood because of its combination of antioxidants, amino acids, and omega fatty acids, which all help to slow the aging process by boosting immune and metabolic function. Chia seeds are rich in polyunsaturated fats, especially omega-3 fatty acids as well as antioxidants and minerals. Raspberries are high in dietary fiber and a good source of vitamin C, B vitamins, folic acid, manganese, copper, magnesium, and iron, all of which help the body function properly.

Ingredients

1 frozen organic banana

1/2 cup frozen organic blueberries

2 tablespoons acai powder

1 teaspoon organic raw honey

1/2 cup almond milk

5 tablespoons vanilla protein powder (plant based)

assorted fresh organic berries and banana (for topping)

hemp seeds (for topping)

chia seeds (for topping)

Preparation

Add frozen banana, blueberries, acai powder, honey, almond milk, and protein powder into a Vitamix or blender and blend until creamy. Pour into a bowl and top with your favorite berries, hemp and chia seeds.

Acai Cleansing Mask

Yerba mate, acai, and honey make this amazing mask a multivitamin for the skin. With over twenty-four vitamins and minerals, and chock full of antioxidants, this mask will make your skin glow. Acai is known as the "beauty berry" because it has so many compounds that make the body look and feel better from the inside out. Its combination of antioxidants, amino acids, and omega fatty acids all help slow the aging process and remove destructive free radicals. Coconut oil is rich in vitamin E, which helps hydrate the skin. The caprylic and lauric acids in coconut oil have antimicrobial and disinfectant properties. The amazing antifungal properties in honey help cleanse skin, fight bacteria, and hydrate dry, damaged skin. Yerba mate helps tighten and tone skin, leaving a youthful glow.

Ingredients

2 tablespoons yerba mate leaves

1/4 teaspoon acai powder

2 organic raspberries, mashed

1 teaspoon coconut oil

1 teaspoon raw organic honey

2 capsules vitamin E oil, reserving 1 capsule for when applying the mask

Preparation

Place yerba mate leaves in 1/4 cup of boiling water and let steep for 20 minutes to make tea. Strain and set brew aside. Combine acai powder, raspberries, coconut oil, and honey in a small pan.

Heat mixture just until it begins to simmer, stirring well. Cool mixture for five minutes and strain through a fine sieve to remove all fruit pieces. Pierce one vitamin E capsule and add to mixture. Stir again and set aside to cool. Mix in yerba mate brew. When cooled, transfer to a small, airtight container or tin.

Usage

Apply a thin layer to face and let set for 5 minutes. Add a small dime-sized amount of water to hands and work wet hands in a circular motion to cleanse. Remove with warm water. Pierce the remaining vitamin E capsule and apply vitamin E oil on face and neck to hydrate skin.

Storage

It can be kept in refrigerator for up to five days. Due to the coconut oil and honey, the mixture will solidify when kept in refrigerator. Simply remove mask and bring it to room temperature before use to make it more pliable.

Green Tea and Cucumber Popsicles

A sweet treat to keep you cool, hydrated, and nourished, these popsicles contain amazing nutrients to help the body function properly. Green tea is an excellent source of antioxidants to help the body fight aging and disease. Cucumbers and mint help with digestion and ward off fatigue.

Ingredients

4 bags green tea (or 1/2 cup loose-leaf green tea)

1 organic cucumber, pureed with skin on

2 teaspoons raw organic honey

1/2 organic lemon, juiced

1/4 cup chopped organic mint

Preparation

Boil 8 cups of filtered water and pour over green tea. Let steep for 20 minutes. If using loose-leaf tea, strain and use only liquid. Mix in pureed cucumber, honey, lemon juice, and mint. Transfer into popsicle containers and freeze for at least 4 hours.

Green Tea and Cucumber Ice Facial and Eye Treatment

A new craze in the beauty world, this ice facial is an amazing anti-aging treatment to get circulation flowing. This chilling experience will leave your skin looking fresh and glowing. Used in many over-the-counter facial products, green tea helps tighten skin and combat wrinkles. Parsley is loaded with vitamin K, which helps with dark circles and improves circulation.

Ingredients

4 bags of green tea (or 1/2 cup loose-leaf green tea)

1/2 organic cucumber, pureed with skin on

1 teaspoon raw organic honey

1/2 cup organic parsley

Preparation

Boil 2 cups of filtered water and pour over green tea. Let steep for 20 minutes. Mix in cucumber, honey, and parsley. Transfer mixture into ice cube tray. Let set for at least 4 hours. Once tray is solid, remove one to two ice cubes from tray. Using either gloves or a washcloth to hold the ice cube, move the ice cube around the face in a circular motion. Be sure to keep ice cubes moving along the face, paying special attention to the under-eye area to relieve puffy eyes. Continue moving around the face for about 5 minutes. Pat dry and apply moisturizer.

Collard Green Wrap with Turmeric Sauce

This delicious raw wrap is easy and nutrient packed, and it can help reduce inflammation. Turmeric, also referred to as the "queen of spices," has a wide range of antioxidant, antiviral, antibacterial, antifungal, anticarcinogenic, and anti-inflammatory properties. It's also loaded with many nutrients, such as protein, dietary fiber, niacin, vitamin C, vitamin E, vitamin K, potassium, calcium, copper, iron, magnesium, and zinc. Turmeric boosts immune health, detoxifies the liver, improves digestion, heals wounds, and much more. The choline in collard greens is an important nutrient that helps with sleep, muscle movement, learning, and memory.

Ingredients

Turmeric Sauce:

1/2 cup fresh coconut milk (refrigerated so it solidifies)

1/4 cup fresh coconut water

1 garlic clove

1/2 teaspoon freshly chopped ginger

2 teaspoons lime juice

1 teaspoon raw honey

1 teaspoon turmeric

pinch Himalayan salt

Wrap:

4 collard green leaves

1/2 red bell pepper, cut into thin strips

1 carrot, cut into thin strips

1 cup cherry tomatoes, cut in half

1/2 cucumber, cut into thin strips

1 cup sprouts

1 avocado

Preparation

For sauce, blend all sauce ingredients in a Vitamix or high-speed blender until smooth. Set aside to let flavors marry.

For wrap, layer vegetable ingredients on collard green leaf and top with turmeric sauce. Roll collard greens, cut in half, and serve.

Brightening Cleansing Grains

Used for centuries, cleansing grains combined natural ingredients to gently exfoliate and remove dirt and oil—a beauty secret passed down for hundreds of years to reveal glowing skin. Turmeric contains curcumin, which is known for its antioxidant and anti-inflammatory properties. There is a long list of benefits associated with turmeric, including the treatment of acne, hyperpigmentation, scars, and other skin conditions, such as eczema and psoriasis. It helps heal dry skin, slows the skin's aging process, diminishes wrinkles, keeps skin supple, and improves skin's elasticity. Cinnamon helps circulation, and kaolin clay draws out impurities in the skin.

Ingredients

1/2 cup almond meal

1/2 cup rose petal powder

1 tablespoon turmeric

1 teaspoon orange peel powder

1/2 cup chickpea flour

1/2 cup kaolin clay

1/2 cup brown rice flour (sifted)

1/2 teaspoon cinnamon

Preparation

Add all ingredients to glass jar. Secure lid and shake to mix.

Usage

Pour a pinch of powder into one hand. Slowly add a small amount of water to powder mixture to create a paste. Using circular motions, cleanse face for 1 minute. Rinse with warm water and splash with cold water. Apply your favorite serum or moisturizer to hydrate skin.

Storage

Keep cleansing grains in glass container with closed lid. It can be stored for up to 6 months.

Tomato-Basil Cucumber Tart

Refreshing and light, this tart will hydrate the body and replenish lost nutrients. Basil is considered one of the healthiest herbs, with a pleasantly pungent flavor and impressive list of nutrients, such as vitamin K, vitamin A, iron, calcium, magnesium, vitamin C, and potassium. Basil also has antibacterial properties and contains DNA-protecting flavonoids. The robust tomato is an excellent source of fiber and vitamins A and C, which help to fight infection. Vitamin K and potassium in tomatoes help to control heart rate and blood pressure. Tomatoes are also rich in vitamin E, thiamin, niacin, vitamin B6, folate, magnesium, phosphorus, and copper, acting as a great multivitamin for the body.

Ingredients

1 cup organic arugula

1 cup organic basil

1/4 cup pine nuts or cashews

2 garlic cloves

2 tablespoons olive oil

black pepper

6 organic red tomatoes

6 organic green tomatoes

6 organic yellow tomatoes

2 large organic cucumbers

pink Himalayan sea salt

Preparation

Line a mini cheesecake pan with parchment paper.

Process arugula, basil, pine nuts, garlic, olive oil, and salt in a food processor or blender into a paste consistency. Place a couple of tablespoons on the bottom of the pan and spread evenly.

Thinly slice all tomatoes and cucumbers. Alternating colors, layer veggies in overlapping spiral pattern. Layer to the top of pan.

Place tomato and cucumber stack in freezer for about five minutes, just long enough to set. Spread a small amount of basil pesto mixture onto plate. Remove stack from pan and place on serving plate.

Top with basil leaves and cracked black pepper.

Tomato-Basil Acne Treatment

This is a great acne spot treatment or toner for the face and body to help combat problematic skin. Tomatoes are a perfect ingredient for combating oily skin, since the acids in tomatoes help to control an oily buildup in the skin's pores. The nourishing properties of tomatoes include vitamins A, C, and K, which will enhance your skin's health. Basil possesses strong antioxidants and is antibacterial and antiviral. It helps to eliminate bacteria and degreases the skin.

Ingredients

1 ripe tomato

2 basil leaves

1/2 cucumber, skin on

Preparation

Combine ingredients in a blender or Vitamix and puree for 30 seconds.

Transfer liquid into a glass container with tight lid.

Usage

Cleanse face, neck, or back and pat dry.

Using a cotton swab or cotton ball, spread tomato mixture on area treating and let dry for 3–5 minutes. Be sure to use a clean cotton ball or swab each time. Rinse with warm water and apply a light moisturizer.

Storage

Refrigerate remaining mixture for up to 5 days. It can be used daily.

Scallops with Avocado-Grapefruit Salsa

Scallops are a great source of vitamin B12 and are a rich source of omega-3 fatty acids, magnesium, and potassium, which assist in cardiovascular health. Rich in vitamins K and B, avocados can help regulate body weight. Grapefruit contains high levels of vitamin C, which is essential for healing wounds, forming cells, and helping proper immune function.

Ingredients

1 organic red grapefruit

1 cup diced avocado (about 1 avocado)

1/4 cup finely diced organic red onion

2 tablespoons chopped organic cilantro

1/2 teaspoon organic lime zest

2 tablespoons fresh organic lime juice

sea salt

freshly ground black pepper

1 tablespoon avocado oil

1 1/2 pounds large sea scallops (about 12)

organic parsley

Preparation

Remove pith and seeds from grapefruit. Slice grapefruit into small chunks.

Add grapefruit, avocado, red onion, cilantro, lime zest, and lime juice to a bowl; gently toss to coat evenly. Season with salt and black pepper to taste.

Heat oil in a large skillet over medium-high heat. Season scallops with salt and black pepper to taste; sear until golden brown and just cooked through, about 2–3 minutes each side.

Transfer scallops to serving plates. Spoon avocado-grapefruit salsa over scallops and top with parsley.

Lightening Acne Mask

Diminish the signs of scars and brown spots caused by acne, hormones, and sun damage with this lightening mask. Manuka honey is known for its high antibacterial properties, which can assist with keeping acne at bay. Rich in vitamins and nutrients, parsley helps brighten skin to reveal a healthy glow. Lemon and grapefruit juices are loaded with healthy vitamins that help exfoliate skin.

Ingredients

1/2 cup fresh flat-leaf parsley

1 teaspoon organic lemon juice**

1 teaspoon organic grapefruit juice

1 tablespoon manuka honey

1 teaspoon kaolin clay

Preparation

Place parsley leaves (stems removed), lemon and grapefruit juices, and honey into a blender or food processor. On low speed, blend for a minute or so until mixture comes together. Using a rubber spatula, remove mixture and place in a glass bowl with lid. Add kaolin clay and mix until a paste is formed.

Usage

Cleanse face with warm water. Apply a layer of mask onto desired areas and let set for 15–20 minutes. Remove with warm water and apply your favorite moisturizer or coconut oil. Discard remaining mask.

**Lemon juice may cause mild tingling sensation. If it becomes uncomfortable, remove mask and cleanse skin with warm water. Avoid direct sun exposure after using this mask.

Artichoke with Lemon-Thyme Dipping Oil

The ancient Greeks considered the artichoke full of health benefits, using it as an aphrodisiac, a diuretic, a breath freshener, and even a deodorant. Rich in fiber, folic acid, and vitamin A, artichokes are not only delicious but also packed with great nutrients. Thyme is antimicrobial and helps the body fight against aliments.

Ingredients

2 whole artichokes

juice of 1 medium lemon

salt

Dipping Sauce:

1/2 cup extra-virgin olive oil

2 tablespoons fresh organic lemon juice

2 teaspoons Dijon mustard

2 teaspoons agave nectar

2 tablespoons finely chopped shallot

2 teaspoons thyme leaves

1 teaspoon fennel seeds

salt and pepper to taste

Preparation

Fill 5-quart saucepan two-thirds full with water. Heat to boiling.

Use a knife to trim the thick stem of each artichoke. Using scissors, snip off tips of leaves.

Rinse artichokes thoroughly with cold running water and transfer them to a pan of boiling water. Add juice of 1 lemon and salt to taste. Cover. Cook over medium-low heat about 45 minutes or until bottoms of artichokes are tender.

Meanwhile, in a small bowl, beat all dipping sauce ingredients with a whisk until emulsified. Pour into dipping bowl and set aside.

Gently remove cooked artichokes from hot water and place upside down on cooling rack to drain for 5 minutes. Turn right side up and transfer to serving plate with dipping sauce. Enjoy.

Lemon, Thyme, and Fennel Cleanser

This antimicrobial cleanser helps keep pimples at bay. Thyme is a natural antiseptic and stabilizes the pH levels in the skin. Fennel seeds help dry out impurities and stimulate blood flow. Lemon is a natural astringent and antiseptic, and it helps to remove dirt and debris from the skin.

Ingredients

1 stem fresh thyme

1 tablespoon fennel seeds

1 tablespoon fresh organic lemon juice

1 cup distilled water

Preparation

To make infusion, drop thyme and fennel seeds into a pot of simmering water. Let them steep like you would when making strong tea, for about 10 minutes.

Remove from heat and strain liquid. Pour liquid into a glass jar or other sealable container. Add lemon juice and mix well.

Usage

Prep skin by wetting face. Soak cotton balls in cooled liquid and apply all over face, neck, and décolleté. Rinse with warm water and apply a nourishing moisturizer. A double cleanse might be needed to remove excess dirt and makeup.

Storage

Keep cleanser in airtight container and store in refrigerator for up to 2 weeks.

Roasted Beet, Avocado, and Grapefruit Salad

This restoring salad calms the mind and feeds the soul. Beets contain betaine, the same substance used in certain treatments of depression. They also contain tryptophan, which relaxes the mind and creates a sense of well-being, similar to chocolate. Avocados contain glutathione, a powerful antioxidant that helps to fight free radicals in the body.

Ingredients

Salad:

4 large organic beets (roasted, peeled, and cubed)

2 cups organic arugula leaves

2 avocados, pitted and cubed

1 1/2 cup organic grapefruit sections, cut into cubes

1/2 cup pine nuts

micro greens (optional)

Dressing:

2 tablespoons organic grapefruit juice

2 tablespoons grade A maple syrup

1/4 teaspoon cumin

1 tablespoon avocado oil

pinch of salt

Preparation

Add all dressing ingredients into a small jar and shake well. Set aside.

To prepare beets, cut off hard ends and rub beets with olive oil. Place on a cookie sheet and bake for about 60 minutes at 350 degrees F until fork tender. Remove from oven and let cool. Peel and cube.

To assemble, divide arugula leaves between four plates. Using a 3-inch ring, place it on top of arugula leaves. Layer each with beets, avocado, and finally grapefruit. Remove ring and drizzle each with dressing. Sprinkle with pine nuts and top with a few micro greens. Enjoy.

Soothing Grapefruit and Avocado Face Mask

This soothing mask calms dry, sensitive skin and reveals healthy-looking skin. Grapefruit and parsley contain immune-enhancing vitamins A and C, and they are powerful antioxidants. Vitamin C not only nourishes the skin but also reduces scars and blemishes. It stimulates the production of collagen, which is the key to cell reproduction and repair. Manuka honey is one of the most powerful and potent kinds of honey available. With its high antibacterial properties, manuka honey helps to treat skin conditions such as acne and eczema. Oatmeal helps to soothe sensitive skin and is a gentle exfoliant to reveal glowing skin.

Ingredients

4 teaspoons organic oatmeal

3 teaspoons organic parsley, chopped

1/2 large organic red grapefruit, juiced

1/2 ripe avocado

2 tablespoons manuka honey

Preparation

Grind oatmeal and parsley in a food processor. Transfer mixture into a bowl and add grapefruit juice. Mix until you have a soft paste. Mash avocado with honey and mix into oatmeal paste. If desired, add one teaspoon of water for a thinner mask.

Usage

Spread soft mixture over face and neck. Let it dry for approximately 15 minutes. Rinse with warm water and apply your favorite moisturizer. Use this face mask once a week for oily skin. Discard remaining mask.

Grapefruit
+
Parsley

Kale Salad with Poached Egg

Kale, nicknamed the "Queen of Greens," is high in iron, vitamin K, and powerful antioxidants. A versatile leafy green makes this salad delicious and nutrient packed. The miracle herb garlic has been used for centuries to flavor food and offer medicinal purposes through its antiviral and antifungal properties. It reduces blood pressure and treats skin conditions, to name just a few benefits.

Ingredients

2 tablespoons avocado oil

1/2 medium organic red onion, sliced

2 garlic cloves, roughly chopped

5 small organic purple sweet potatoes

1 large bunch organic kale, chopped

1 cup organic cherry tomatoes, cut in half

1/4 teaspoon salt

1/4 teaspoon pepper

2 eggs

Preparation

Heat oil in a large pan over medium heat. Add onion, garlic, and potatoes, cooking for about 15 minutes until potatoes are soft.

Fill a pot with a few inches of water. Add a splash of vinegar. Heat water until just before simmer (no bubbles). Add eggs, one at a time, into water and cook for 3–4 minutes, pushing sides in to help eggs set. Remove with slotted spoon and set aside.

Add kale and tomatoes to potato mixture and sauté for 3 minute, seasoning with salt and pepper.

Transfer potato mixture to two plates. Top each with poached egg and serve.

Kale Firming Mask and Eye Treatment

Tired, aged skin gets a boost with this powerhouse duo treatment, resulting in a perfect glow. Kelp powder is rich in proteins, minerals, and vitamins, including vitamin B12 and vitamin E. It acts as a powerful detoxifier, which draws out toxins and impurities while adding beneficial nutrients. Kale's antioxidants are a great way to reduce wrinkles because they help to prevent free-radical cell damage to skin. The lactic acid in yogurt exfoliates dead skin cells. Avocado oil and honey help lock in moisture and hydrate dry skin. Rich in proteins, egg whites help tighten the skin around the eyes and reduce the appearance of fine lines.

Ingredients

Face Mask:

1/4 cup organic kale

1 teaspoon avocado oil

2 tablespoons plain organic yogurt

1 teaspoon organic kelp powder

1 teaspoon raw organic honey

Eye Treatment:

1 egg white

1/2 lemon, juiced

Preparation

In a food processor or blender, quickly pulse kale and oil to a thick paste consistency and pour into a small dish. Add yogurt and kelp powder; mix well. Add honey to mixture and stir until smooth.

Using a mixer, beat egg white and lemon juice until stiff peaks form.

Usage

Cleanse face and apply egg mixture around eye area, avoiding eyes. Apply kale mask all over face, neck, and shoulder area. Massage lightly in a circular motion, leaving on for 10 minutes. Remove mask and eye treatment with a warm washcloth. Wash face and apply your favorite moisturizer as usual. Skin will be glowing and refreshed.

Tangy Carrot Salad

Tangy and delicious, this salad is bursting with flavor and nutrients for the entire body. Goji berries, loaded with vitamins and minerals, are an amazing anti-inflammatory. Carrots are well known for their vitamin A, which helps to improve vision, promotes healthy skin, and cleanses the body. Organic apple cider vinegar is antibacterial, antiviral, and antifungal. It has many uses—from cleaning the house to curing a sore throat, healing heartburn, increasing energy, and so much more.

Ingredients

1 1/2 tablespoons raw, unfiltered apple cider vinegar

1 small garlic clove, minced

2 cups grated organic carrots

1/2 organic apple, diced

1/4 cup sliced organic green onions

1/4 cup freshly chopped organic parsley

1/4 cup chopped goji berries (soaked in water for 15 minutes)

1 teaspoon organic raw honey

1 tablespoon olive oil

salt and pepper to taste

2 cups organic baby spinach leaves

Preparation

Combine vinegar and garlic in a small bowl. Let stand 15 minutes.

Stir together carrots, apple, green onions, parsley, and goji berries in a large bowl. Whisk together honey, oil, and apple cider vinegar mixture. Pour vinaigrette over carrot mixture; toss to coat. Season with salt and pepper.

Cover and chill for at least 2 hours. Serve carrot salad over spinach leaves.

Carrot and Goji Facial Cleanser

Truly the cream of the crop, this cleanser balances skin's pH, removes built-up oil, and tightens pores. Carrots contain a large amount of beta-carotene, which, when entering the body, changes into vitamin A and reduces cell degeneration, slowing down the aging process. It improves the amount of collagen in the skin, helps maintain elasticity, and reduces the signs of aging. Goji berries are loaded with vitamin C and anti-inflammatory and antifungal properties that help fight the signs of aging and keep skin clean. Apple cider vinegar helps regulate skin's pH, is antifungal, which keeps those pesky pimples at bay, and can help fade dark spots.

Ingredients

3/4 cup fresh organic carrot juice

1 tablespoon dried goji berries

1/2 teaspoon raw, unfiltered apple cider vinegar

Preparation

Soak goji berries in carrot juice for 30 minutes. Transfer softened goji berries and carrot juice into a high-power blender. Add apple cider vinegar and blend until smooth and liquid.

Transfer cleanser into spray bottle or glass container with lid.

Usage

Wet face with warm water and dip cotton balls in cleanser. In a circular motion, cleanse face, neck, and décolleté. Splash with cool water. Apply either coconut oil or your favorite moisturizer for further hydration.

Storage

Store unused cleanser in refrigerator for up to 5 days.

Raw Superfood Balls

These small bites pack a truckload of nutrients and will give you energy and stamina all day. Maca is an endocrine adaptogen, which nourishes the entire endocrine system, strengthening the adrenals, supporting hormonal balance, and increasing stamina and vitality. Cacao is full of magnesium and is one of the richest antioxidant foods on the planet. It's also a great source for tryptophan and serotonin to keep one calm and happy.

Ingredients

1 cup pitted Medjool dates (about 10)

1/2 cup raw cashews

1/2 cup raw almonds

1/4 cup cacao powder

1 teaspoon chia seeds

1 teaspoon pure vanilla extract

2 tablespoons maca powder

1/3 cup coconut oil

3 or 4 tablespoons unsweetened dried and shredded coconut (optional)

Preparation

Soak dates and nuts in filtered water for 30 minutes and drain them fully. Add all ingredients except coconut shreds into blender and blend well. Let sit for 10 minutes, then mold into ball shapes before covering with shredded coconut.

Vitality Facial Scrub

Give skin a vitamin boost with this antioxidant-packed exfoliating scrub. When topically applied, these amazing superfoods are high in regenerative essential fatty acids, proteins, vitamins, and minerals, which will improve the overall texture and tone of the skin. Maca can help improve the overall skin tone. Skin will become luminous and healthy after using this vitality scrub.

Ingredients

1/2 cup maca powder

1/4 cup coconut flour

1/2 cup kaolin clay

1/2 cup finely granulated coconut sugar

1 tablespoon raw cacao powder

Preparation

Mix all ingredients in a glass jar with tight lid. Shake to blend.

Usage

Pour a small amount into palm and mix with about one tablespoon of water to make a paste, adding more for your desired consistency. Using circular motions, lightly scrub face, neck, and décolleté. To remove, rinse with warm water and apply your favorite serum or moisturizer to lock in hydration. Dry powder can be stored for up to 1 year.

Invigorating Peppermint-Orange Tea

This is an invigorating drink that helps boost clarity and awakens the mind. A great alternative to coffee, yerba mate helps to keep you alert and provides your body with all the nutrients needed to sustain life, including twenty-four vitamins and minerals, and fifteen amino acids. Peppermint and orange help to elevate mood while adding a hint of flavor.

Ingredients

1/2 tablespoon dried orange peel

1/2 tablespoon chopped dried mint

2 tablespoons yerba mate tea

16 ounces filtered water

organic raw honey to taste

fresh organic orange peel

Preparation

Mix dried orange peel, mint, and yerba mate tea in a bowl. Boil water and pour over tea mixture, allowing it to steep for 5 minutes. Strain and transfer into two 8-ounce cups. Add honey and orange peel. Enjoy.

Youthful Eye Treatment

Tired eyes are rejuvenated and looking fresh with this pick-me-up eye treatment. Yerba mate is packed with amazing antioxidants, amino acids, vitamins, and minerals to bring a youthful glow to skin. This eye treatment gets a boost from honey to increase circulation and help moisturize skin. Parsley is loaded with vitamin K to help reduce the appearance of dark circles.

Ingredients

1 tablespoon loose-leaf yerba mate

1/2 teaspoon organic parsley

1/2 teaspoon organic mint

1 tablespoon ground flax meal

1/3 teaspoon flaxseed oil

1 teaspoon manuka honey

Preparation

Using a coffee grinder, grind yerba mate, parsley, and mint. Place yerba mate mixture and flax meal in a mixing bowl. Bring 1/4 cup water to boil and pour over mixture. Stir and let steep for 5 minutes. Next, add flaxseed oil and honey. Stir to create a thick paste. If needed, add a small amount of flax meal to thicken.

Usage

Start with clean skin. Spread a thin layer of paste under eye area and allow to penetrate for 15 minutes. Rinse with warm water to remove and finish with application of coconut oil around the orbital area. Store remainder of paste in a sealed container and use within 3 days.

Forbidden Black Rice with Shrimp

This delicious meal helps to combat inflammation and boosts overall health. Ginger is one of the most ancient spices in worldwide cuisine. It has become well known for its various health benefits, which include its ability to boost bone health, strengthen the immune system, aid digestion, eliminate arthritis symptoms, and relieve pains related to menstrual disorders, nausea, and flu. Shrimp are an unusually concentrated source of the antioxidant and anti-inflammatory nutrient called "astaxanthin." Astaxanthin is a carotenoid known for its anti-inflammatory and antioxidant properties. Bragg Liquid Aminos is a wonderful source of naturally occurring amino acids and is a great alternative to soy sauce.

Ingredients

2 cups organic coconut milk

1 cup organic black rice

1 tablespoon Bragg Liquid Aminos

1 tablespoon sesame oil

2 tablespoons chopped organic ginger

2 tablespoons chopped organic garlic

4 tablespoons chopped organic green onion

1 organic red bell pepper, chopped

1/2 pound large shrimp

1/4 cup organic edamame

1/2 organic lime, juiced

2 tablespoons chopped organic cilantro

Preparation

Combine coconut milk and rice in a saucepan and bring to boil. Cover, reduce heat, and simmer for 30 minutes. Let stand for a few minutes, then fluff with a fork.

In a medium skillet, warm Bragg Liquid Aminos and sesame oil over medium heat. Add ginger, garlic, green onions, red pepper, shrimp, and edamame. Sauté for 5 minutes or until shrimp is cooked. Remove from heat.

In a large bowl, combine shrimp sauté with rice and mix well. Squeeze lime juice over mixture and sprinkle with cilantro.

Black Rice and Ginger-Coconut Scrub

Give your skin a vibrant glow with this exotic scrub, which is rich in emollients and antioxidants. Ginger's antioxidant gingerol not only fights skin-damaging free radicals but also promotes smoothness and evenness in skin tone and increases circulation. Coconut oil is rich in fatty acids, such as capric acid, caprylic acid, and lauric acid. The fatty acids have disinfectant and antimicrobial properties. Coconut oil is high in vitamin E, which is known for its skin-healing properties. The triglycerides in coconut oil help to keep moisture from escaping from the skin, which aids in retaining softness and suppleness.

Ingredients

1/2 cup organic black rice

1 teaspoon ginger, freshly grated

1 teaspoon sesame oil

1/4 cup coconut oil, slightly warmed to a liquid state

Preparation

In a food processor or blender, pulse rice for 15 seconds into coarse pieces. Combine ginger, sesame and coconut oil in glass-free container. Add rice and mix well.

Usage

Take scrub into a hot shower and apply to skin, using a circular motion begin with feet and work up to shoulders, exfoliating the body.

Rinse thoroughly and pat dry. Apply warmed coconut oil to body for extra hydration. It can be used up to two times per week to reveal radiant, smooth skin.

Storage

Store scrub in airtight container up to 10 days. Warm slightly before using.

Gluten Free Coffee-Carob Chip Biscotti

This delicious snack boosts energy and curbs your sweet tooth craving. Pumpkin seeds have large amounts of vitamins and minerals including copper, iron, zinc, vitamin K, manganese, magnesium, and phosphorus. Coconut oil contains a unique combination of fatty acids with powerful medicinal properties. It contains lauric acids, which aid digestion, is antiviral, and boosts energy.

Ingredients

2 cups almond flour

3/4 cup coconut flour

1 cup organic coconut sugar

2 teaspoons baking powder

1 teaspoon cinnamon

1/4 teaspoon sea salt

2 tablespoons finely ground coffee

1 cup carob chips

1/4 cup pumpkin seeds

2 tablespoons coconut oil

2 teaspoons pure vanilla extract

3 large eggs

Preparation

Preheat oven to 350 degrees F. Coat baking sheet with coconut oil.

Combine all dry ingredients in a bowl. In a separate bowl, combine oil, vanilla, and eggs. Add dry ingredients to wet ingredients and stir until blended well. The dough will be very dry.

Knead the dough until it comes together. Divide the dough in half and shape into two logs about eight inches long each, then flatten to about one inch thick. Place on baking sheet three inches apart and bake for 35 minutes. Remove and brush lightly with water, letting cool for 5 minutes before cutting.

Cut biscotti into 3/4-inch slices and place on baking sheet. Bake at 325 degrees F for 10 minutes on each side. Remove and cool before serving.

Energizing Coffee Scrub

This invigorating scrub reduces the appearance of cellulite and energizes the mind, body, and spirit. The caffeine and antioxidants in coffee work to tighten and energize skin while also promoting circulation. This gives it the ability to smooth skin and reduce the appearance of cellulite. Coconut oil is loaded with healing benefits for the skin and improves the condition of the skin in a number of ways. Its high moisture-retaining capacity helps to prevent skin from drying out, and it nourishes skin deep down. Its antioxidant properties help to combat the effects of harmful free radicals, and its antibacterial and antifungal capabilities help to reduce the risk of infections.

Ingredients

1/4 cup coarse ground coffee

1/4 cup sea salt

1/4 cup organic coconut sugar

3/4 cup organic coconut oil, warmed

1/4 cup flaxseed oil

lemon zest

4 mint leaves, chopped

peppermint essential oil (optional)

Preparation

In a bowl mix ground coffee, sea salt, and sugar. Add coconut oil, flaxseed oil, lemon zest, mint and peppermint oil. Mix well.

Usage

In the shower, massage mixture in a circular motion all over body, paying close attention to hip, thigh, and stomach area. Allow scrub to rest for 5 minutes to penetrate into skin, then rinse with warm water. Towel dry and apply warm coconut oil to further hydrate and repair dry skin.

To maximize the benefits of the scrub, use a dry brush or dry washcloth on skin in a circular motion before applying scrub. This will help stimulate circulation and drain lymphatic system of toxins.

Note, this scrub is very messy, so make sure to use in the shower.

Storage

Store scrub in airtight container at room temperature. This scrub will keep for up to 1 month.

Avocado-Papaya Salad

This light, refreshing salad is great for lunch. Add wild salmon for a protein-packed dinner. Avocados are high in vitamin B6 and natural folic acid as well as healthy omega-3 fatty acids and vitamin E. Papayas are particularly high in vitamins A, C, and E; all are powerful immune-boosting antioxidant vitamins. Papayas are well known for their high enzyme content, which helps the food to break down rapidly without much extra work required from the body. Among the many health benefits of honey, it can be a powerful immune system booster. Its antioxidant and antibacterial properties can help improve the digestive system and help people stay healthy.

Ingredients

Dressing:

2 organic limes, juiced

1 tablespoon dark organic honey

1/4 teaspoon sea salt

1/4 teaspoon freshly cracked black pepper

2 tablespoon organic cilantro, chopped

1 garlic clove, finely chopped

3 tablespoons olive oil

Salad:

2 organic avocados

4 cups mixed organic baby lettuce greens

1 organic papaya

Preparation

Combine lime juice, honey, salt, and pepper. Blend until smooth. Add chopped cilantro, garlic, and olive oil. Mix and set aside.

Peel papaya and cut in half. Using a spoon, remove and discard seeds. Slice papaya halves into thin strips. Cut avocados in half and remove pits and skin. Slice avocado into strips.

Add dressing mixture to salad greens, tossing well to coat evenly. Mound a portion of greens in the center of each plate. Arrange papaya and avocado over greens. Drizzle with remaining dressing and sprinkle with chopped cilantro.

Avocado-Papaya Face and Body Mask

Great for all skin types, this simple mask works to exfoliate, hydrate, and nourish dry skin. Avocado health benefits make it considered one of nature's most effective moisturizers, and it has been shown to increase collagen production and reduce the appearance of wrinkles. Papayas are a good source of vitamin A and papain, which helps in removing dead skin cells and breaking down inactive protein. Raw honey is incredible for your skin thanks to its antibacterial properties and a hefty serving of skin-saving antioxidants.

Ingredients

1 ripe organic avocado

1/4 ripe organic papaya

2 tablespoons dark organic honey

plastic wrap

Preparation

Peel avocado and papaya, taking out pits and seeds. In a bowl, mash avocado and papaya into a smooth paste. Add honey, stir, and set aside.

Usage

Prepare a large towel or sheet over your desired area of rest.

Prep skin by using either a dry brush or loofah in a circular motion over the body to exfoliate dead skin. Spread mask over face and body in a circular motion.

Starting at your feet, wrap each leg with plastic wrap. Work your way up to your chest and each arm, wrapping in plastic wrap or warm towel. Avoid neck and head area. Lie down and relax for 15 minutes.

Remove plastic wrap and rinse body with warm water. Finally, apply a soothing lotion or coconut oil to further hydrate skin.

Pumpkin-Sage Quinoa

This unique blend is bursting with flavor and loaded with nutrients to recharge and energize. Maca is well known for its ability to help energize the body due to its large amount of B vitamins. Pumpkin is high in fiber and beta-carotene, which helps maintain healthy, glowing skin. Sage aids in digestion and is anti-inflammatory.

Ingredients

1 tablespoon avocado oil

3 cups pumpkin, chopped into 1-inch chunks

1 cup organic quinoa

1 organic yellow onion, finely chopped

1 garlic clove, minced

1/2 teaspoon salt and pepper

4 organic sage leaves

1 teaspoon maca powder

pumpkin seeds

Preparation

Warm oil in a pan over medium heat. Add pumpkin and cook for 10 minutes. Meanwhile, wash and strain quinoa and cook according to package.

Add onion, garlic, salt, pepper, and sage to pumpkin. Cook until onions are translucent. Remove from heat and stir in maca powder.

Mix pumpkin mixture with quinoa. Top with pumpkin seeds and sage. Serve.

Anti-Aging Pumpkin Clay Skin Healer

Healing clays like bentonite have a high concentration of minerals including silica, calcium, magnesium, sodium, iron, and potassium. These minerals help pull toxins from the body. Pumpkin is packed with fruit enzymes and alpha hydroxy acids (AHAs), which increase cell turnover and brighten and smooth the skin. They also contain antioxidants, vitamin A, and vitamin C to help soften and soothe the skin, and boost collagen production to prevent signs of aging. There are a variety of antioxidants in olive oil, including vitamins A and E, but the most potent compound is hydroxytyrosol. Hydroxytyrosol is a very rare but potent antioxidant found in olive oil, which prevents free-radical damage on skin cells.

Ingredients

1/2 cup organic pumpkin puree

1/4 cup bentonite clay (available at health food stores)

4 tablespoons manuka honey

2 tablespoons purified or coconut water

1 tablespoon coconut oil

1 teaspoon maca powder

2 sage leaves, chopped into small pieces

Preparation

Mix all ingredients in a large bowl. Mixture should have a paste-like consistency.

Usage

Prep the skin by using a loofah or dry washcloth in a circular motion to exfoliate skin. Apply mask to body and let set for 20 minutes. To enhance penetration of mask, wrap body in plastic wrap. Simply wrap legs, stomach, and arms.

Rinse off mask with warm water and apply either coconut oil or olive oil to hydrate skin and leave it looking silky and glowing.

Storage

Transfer mixture into airtight container and store in refrigerator for up 5 days. It can be used twice a week.

Pure Bliss Herbal Tea

This calming tea will take you to a state of pure bliss. Sage and lavender help boost alertness and mood while decreasing anxiety. Sea buckthorn is probably one of the top nutritious fruits. This ancient fruit contains 190 active nutrients, including vitamins A, B1, B2, C, D, E, and K; carotenoids; flavonoids; amino acids; phenols; folic acid; and twenty different minerals.

Ingredients

1/4 cup dried pineapple

3–4 pieces chopped dried apple

4 pieces dried oranges, sliced

1/2 teaspoon dried culinary lavender

1/2 teaspoon dried sage

tea strainer or bags

3–4 drops sea buckthorn oil

Preparation

Mix all ingredients except sea buckthorn oil in a tea bag or strainer and place in a pot of hot water. Let steep 8–10 minutes. Pour desired cup of tea and add a few drops of sea buckthorn oil to each cup.

Herbal Relaxing Bath Soak

Bath time has never been so relaxing. Lavender and sage help soothe the soul and reduce anxiety. Sea buckthorn oil helps nourish the skin and combats skin conditions such as eczema and rosacea. The minerals and nutrients in Himalayan salts can improve skin texture and tone, combat water retention, and promote sinus health. Himalayan salts can also prevent muscle cramps, regulate sleep, and decrease stress.

Ingredients

1/2 cup chopped herbs (sage and lavender)

1/4 cup dried orange peel

1/4 cup dried pineapple

1/2 cup Himalayan salt

1 teaspoon sea buckthorn oil

sachet

Preparation

Add herbs, fruit, and salt in bowl. Add sea buckthorn oil and mix well. Store in airtight container.

Usage

Scoop a small amount of bath soak into sachet. Draw a warm bath and place sachet directly under running water to infuse water with herbal mixture. Relax in bath for at least 15 minutes. To enhance your experience, use chilled chamomile tea bags or cucumber slices over eyes.

Storage

Store bath soak in airtight container. Discard after 2 months.

Watermelon Salad

Hydrating and refreshing, this salad is loaded with flavor and nutrients, and it brings the feeling of summer. Watermelon is rich in phenolic compounds, such as flavonoids, carotenoids, and triterpenoids. The carotenoid lycopene in watermelon is particularly beneficial in reducing inflammation and neutralizing free radicals. Peppermint is a good source of manganese, copper, and vitamin C, which helps to keep the immune system strong.

Ingredients

1/4 cup extra-virgin olive oil

3 tablespoons fresh organic lemon juice

2 teaspoons sea salt

1/2 teaspoon freshly ground pepper

1 (8-pound) seedless watermelon, cut into 1-inch chunks (10 cups)

1/2 cup feta cheese, crumbled (optional)

1 small red onion, cut into 1/2-inch dice

1 cup chopped mint leaves

Preparation

In a large bowl, whisk oil, lemon juice, salt, and pepper. Add watermelon, feta, onion and mint. Toss gently. Garnish with mint and serve.

Watermelon-Hydrating Skin Healer

Whether you've been in the sun too long and are a little crisp or your skin is just parched from the hot weather, this instant skin healer will work magic. Watermelon is known for its high water content and amazing vitamins, such as C and B6, which help hydrate and moisturize the skin. Honey and coconut milk help to lock in moisture and further hydrate and nourish, leaving skin repaired and protected.

Ingredients

2 tablespoons fresh watermelon juice

1 tablespoon raw honey

2 tablespoons coconut milk

Preparation

Mix watermelon juice, honey, and coconut milk.

Usage

Apply serum to clean skin and allow to absorb for 15–20 minutes. Remove with cool water and hydrate skin. Store in refrigerator in sealed container for up to 10 days.

Roasted Veggies with Cayenne Pepper

Hot and spicy, cayenne pepper adds zest to this flavorful dish and health benefits to those brave enough to risk its fiery heat. The hotness cayenne produces is caused by its high concentration of capsaicin. Capsaicin is known for its pain-reducing effects, cardiovascular benefits, and ability to help prevent ulcers. Capsaicin also effectively opens and drains congested nasal passages. In addition to their high capsaicin content, cayenne peppers are also an excellent source of vitamin A. Mushrooms are packed with vitamin D, which is vital for the body to function properly and helps fight disease.

Ingredients

1 organic red bell pepper, chopped

1 organic yellow bell pepper, chopped

1 bunch organic asparagus tips

1 package organic mushrooms

1 medium organic red onion, chopped

1 cup chopped organic carrots

2 cups cubed organic sweet potatoes

1 crushed garlic clove

avocado oil

3–4 tablespoons cayenne pepper

salt and pepper to taste

Preparation

Preheat oven to 350 degrees F.

In a medium-sized bowl, add all vegetables and garlic. Toss with oil until well coated. Sprinkle mixture with cayenne pepper, salt, and pepper. Mix well to coat all veggies.

Spread mixture onto a baking sheet and bake for 45 minutes to 1 hour, turning twice during baking process. Serve warm.

Cayenne Pepper Pain-Relief Cream

A holistic approach to pain, this cream will help alleviate sore joints and muscles. Cayenne pepper contains capsaicin, which helps to relieve pain. Capsaicin works by first stimulating and then decreasing the intensity of pain signals in the body. Although pain may increase at first, it usually decreases after the first use. Capsaicin stimulates the release of a compound believed to be involved in communicating pain between the nerves in the spinal cord and other parts of the body. This is a great pain-management treatment for those who suffer with chronic pain, arthritis, and other ailments. Shea butter and coconut oil help hydrate and nourish the skin.

Ingredients

4 tablespoons cayenne pepper

1/2 cup coconut oil

1/2 cup shea butter

Glass container with tight-fitting lid

Preparation

In a double boiler, mix cayenne pepper and oil over medium heat for 5 minutes. Add in shea butter, mixing thoroughly and heating until everything is melted.

Chill mixture for 15 minutes. Stir and return to refrigerator for another 15 minutes. Remove from refrigerator and beat with a hand mixer for 10 minutes or until peak forms. Transfer to glass container with tight-fitting lid. Store in refrigerator.

Usage

Apply a small amount daily on areas that need pain relief, such as hands, feet, joints, and lower back. It is normal to feel a tingling sensation. Avoid eye area. Keep away from small children.

Storage

Keep in refrigerator for up to 3 months. Remove a spoonful at a time when ready to use.

Turmeric-Ginger Dip

This healthy snack or simple appetizer is sure to please a crowd and deliver a boost of goodness to your body. Turmeric is a super spice with a high-antioxidant value that boosts the immune system. It is a powerful anti-inflammatory and is a popular spice not only for cooking but also for home remedies. For thousands of years, Arabic, Indian, and Asian healers prized ginger as both food and medicine. This tropical plant, in the same family as turmeric, is effectively used to relieve nausea and vomiting caused by illness and seasickness.

Ingredients

1 cup raw cashews, soaked

1 tablespoon extra-virgin olive oil

2 garlic cloves

1/4 cup coconut milk

1 tablespoon turmeric

1 teaspoon ginger

1 tablespoon honey

Organic sweet potatoes

Organic cucumber slices

Organic carrot sticks

Organic sugar snap pea pods

Organic celery sticks

Organic radishes

Organic cherry tomatoes

Organic brussels sprouts

Organic asparagus

Preparation

Cover cashews in water and soak at least 4 hours. Drain cashews and transfer to a blender. Add olive oil, garlic, coconut milk, turmeric, ginger, and honey. Blend until smooth. Set aside.

Roast sweet potatoes, brussels sprouts, and asparagus until cooked but crisp. Serve dip with roasted veggies and cucumber slices, carrots, peas, celery, radishes, and cherry tomatoes.

Turmeric and Ginger Stretch Mark Oil

This multivitamin oil combines ancient healing properties to help heal damaged skin. Wheat germ is loaded with vitamin E, which helps to boost skin's elasticity and reduces free-radical damage. Both ginger and turmeric are well known for their collagen-boosting properties, which help repair damaged skin. Coconut oil hydrates and nourishes the skin; it is rich in fatty acids, which help skin texture and tone. Over time, skin becomes smooth and rejuvenated.

Ingredients

2 cups wheat germ oil

1 cup coconut oil

1 cup chopped fresh ginger

1 cup chopped fresh turmeric

Preparation

In a double boiler, combine all ingredients and bring to a simmer. Reduce heat to low and cook for 20 minutes. Strain oil mixture to remove ginger and turmeric pieces. Transfer to airtight container.

Usage

When ready to use, slightly warm oil. To increase blood flow, use a dry brush or dry washcloth in a circular motion on problematic area for 2 minutes. Apply oil to skin in a circular massaging motion to increase circulation and blood flow to targeted area. For maximum benefit, use twice per day.

Storage

Keep at room temperature in airtight container. Use within 2 months.

Avocado-Cacao Pudding

Here's a heavenly treat to calm your sweet tooth without feeling guilty. Avocados are considered some of the healthiest foods on the planet, because they contain twenty-five essential nutrients, including vitamin A, B, C, E, and K; copper; iron; phosphorus; magnesium; and potassium. Avocados also contain fiber, protein, and several beneficial phytochemicals, such as beta-sitosterol, glutathione, and lutein, which may protect against various disease and illness. Maca packs a powerful punch, providing energy and stamina, and it also aids in increasing low libido. Raw cacao is loaded with antioxidants that help keep the body functioning properly.

Ingredients

2 ripe organic avocados

1/4 cup raw cacao powder

1/4 cup melted cacao nibs

1 tablespoon maca powder

3 tablespoons raw organic honey

1 teaspoon coconut oil

1 teaspoon vanilla

dash of salt

raspberries for garnish

mint leaves for garnish

Try adding a dash of cayenne pepper or cinnamon for a little kick.

Preparation

In a food processor or Vitamix, combine all ingredients except mint and raspberries. Blend for several minutes until smooth and shiny.

Transfer to small ramekins. Refrigerate for at least 4 hours and garnish with raspberries and fresh mint leaves.

Hydrating Avocado-Cacao Body Mask

Getting dirty with your food has never been so much fun. Cacao is packed with antioxidants, which help block harmful free radicals. It contains skin-protecting vitamins, such as magnesium and vitamin C. Avocados are rich in omega fatty acids, which promote cellular repair and rejuvenation.

Ingredients

2 ripe organic avocados

2 tablespoons cacao powder

2 tablespoons raw organic honey

1 tablespoon maca powder

Preparation

Blend all ingredients into smooth paste.

Usage

Apply to body and face. Leave on for 15–20 minutes. Rinse with warm water and apply coconut oil to further hydrate skin. Discard remaining mask.

A fun treat for a group of friends: apply mask to body and let harden or "bake" in the sun for 20–30 minutes.

Monster Green Smoothie

One of my favorite morning rituals, this superfood-packed smoothie will leave you bursting with energy and feeling great for the entire day. Spirulina is recognized as one of the world's most nutritionally complete superfood, since it offers health benefits to practically every organ and body function. Dandelion greens are high in calcium and rich in iron. They have been eaten for thousands of years to treat anemia, skin problems, blood disorders, and depression.

Ingredients

1/4 cup organic spinach

1/4 cup organic kale

1/4 cup dandelion greens

1/4 cup organic rainbow chard

1 organic apple, chopped

1 organic banana

1 cup chopped pineapple

1 teaspoon spirulina powder

1 teaspoon aloe vera

1 cup coconut water

1 tablespoon coconut oil

1 tablespoon chia seeds

Preparation

Place spinach, kale, dandelion greens, rainbow chard, apple, banana, pineapple, spirulina powder, and aloe vera in blender or Vitamix.

Add coconut water and coconut oil. Blend until smooth, about 45 seconds. Add in chia seeds and mix for 10 seconds. Transfer to three 8-ounce cups. Enjoy.

Detoxifying Spirulina Face and Body Mask

This simple yet powerful mask helps to improve skin texture and tone, leaving it refreshed and glowing. Spirulina prevents premature skin aging, improves skin function and overall appearance, and helps in the fight against acne. The Egyptians and other cultures have used aloe vera for centuries to soothe skin conditions and even skin tone.

Ingredients

1 teaspoon chia seeds

1 teaspoon coconut water

2 teaspoons spirulina powder or Organifi Green Juice Powder

1/2 teaspoon aloe vera

1 tablespoon manuka honey

2 tablespoons full-fat yogurt

Preparation

Soak chia seeds in coconut water for 25 minutes until gel forms.

Mix spirulina powder, aloe vera, honey, and yogurt until smooth. Add in chia seeds and mix well.

Usage

In the shower, prep skin by dry brushing the body for two minutes. Apply mask to clean face and body, allowing it to rest on skin for about 15 minutes. You can create a steam shower experience by turning up the heat and allowing the shower to run just adjacent to your body so that the steam helps the mask to penetrate the skin. Make sure, however, you are mindful of wasting water.

Rinse with warm water, pat dry, and apply coconut oil to further enhance this nourishing mask. Discard leftover mask.

Power Granola Bars

Great for snacks or a simple breakfast on the go, these power granola bars will keep you functioning all day. Maca powder and pumpkin seeds give you sustainable energy and endurance. Bananas and chia seeds are packed with antioxidants to keep the body functioning properly.

Ingredients

1 1/2 cups mashed ripe organic banana

1 teaspoon pure vanilla extract

2 tablespoons raw organic honey

1/3 cup almond butter

1 tablespoon coconut oil

1/4 teaspoon pink Himalayan salt

1 teaspoon cinnamon

1 teaspoon maca powder

2 tablespoons chia seeds

1 1/2 cups organic rolled oats (gluten free)

1 cup organic buckwheat groats

1/3 cup dried cherries, chopped

1/3 cup sunflower seeds

1/3 cup pepita seeds

Directions

Preheat oven to 350 degrees F. Lightly grease a large rectangular baking dish (approx. 8.5 inches by 12.5 inches). Line dish with parchment paper so bars are easier to lift out.

In a medium saucepan, heat mashed banana, vanilla, honey, almond butter, coconut oil, salt, and cinnamon until just melted and smooth. Remove from heat and add maca and chia seeds.

Place rolled oats into a food processor and pulse until they are coarsely chopped (but still with lots of texture). Stir oats and buckwheat groats into banana mixture.

Add chopped dried cherries, sunflower seeds, and pepita seeds into banana-oat mixture. Mix until thoroughly combined.

Spoon mixture into prepared dish. Press down with spatula until compacted, smooth, and even.

Bake for about 15–20 minutes until firm and lightly golden along edges. Place dish on a cooling rack for 10 minutes. Carefully slide knife to loosen ends and lift out. Place granola slab on cooling rack for about 15 minutes. Once granola is cool, slice it into squares.

After-Sun Skin Healer

After a day in the sun, skin is dry and sensitive. This after-sun paste nourishes the skin with vital nutrients found in oatmeal, yogurt, and bananas. The polysaccharides in oatmeal cool and heal skin. Live cultured, plain yogurt contains an abundance of probiotics and enzymes that help to soothe and heal. Potassium in bananas hydrates and nourishes dehydrated skin.

Ingredients

1 ripe banana

4 tablespoons manuka honey

1/4 cup organic full-fat yogurt

1 cup finely ground oatmeal

Preparation

Mash banana in a small bowl. Add honey and yogurt. Slowly add in finely ground oatmeal and mix until a smooth paste is formed.

Usage

Apply oatmeal paste to face and body, leaving on for 10 minutes. Remove with warm water and apply a hydrating lotion or aloe to soothe skin.

Storage

Store in refrigerator in airtight container. Discard after two days.

Cucumber-Melon Mojito

Staying hydrated doesn't mean you need to drink only water. Cucumbers are 95 percent water; they keep the body hydrated while helping the body to eliminate toxins. Don't forget to leave the skin on, because it contains a good amount of vitamin C, about 10 percent of the daily-recommended allowance. Honeydew melon is high in copper, vitamin C, and vitamin B6; these help the body to regenerate new skin cells.

Ingredients

1 organic lime

3 sprigs fresh organic mint

3 (1 1/2-inch-long) pieces organic cucumber, sliced crosswise into 6 pieces

4 teaspoons raw sugar

2 cups crushed ice

1 cup fresh honeydew melon juice

sparkling mineral water

cucumber for garnish

mint for garnish

Vodka (optional)

Preparation

Place lime, mint, cucumber slices, and sugar in a tumbler or highball glass and muddle.

Add ice to glass. If adding vodka, pour 2 shots over ice. Pour honeydew melon juice over ice and top with sparkling mineral water. Stir and serve immediately, garnished with cucumber and mint.

Mojito Foot Soak and Scrub

This foot soak helps to rejuvenate and heal tired feet, putting a little pep back in your step. Enzymes from lime juice help to remove dead skin while witch hazel helps to alleviate swelling. Epsom salts help to relax tired, sore feet and pull out toxins. Feet are left soft and revived.

Ingredients

1/2 cup witch hazel

1/2 cup freshly squeezed lime juice

1/2 cup freshly squeezed honeydew melon juice

1 lime sliced into rings

1/2 cup fresh mint leaves

1/2 cup Epsom salts

1/2 quart sparkling mineral water at room temperature

4 cups hot water

2 tablespoons raw sugar

1 tablespoon coconut oil, warmed to liquid state

Preparation

Mix witch hazel, lime juice, honeydew melon juice, and lime rings into a bowl large enough to soak your feet. Mash mint leaves with the back of a spoon, then tear into big pieces, adding to the mixture. Add Epsom salts and sparkling water. Finally add hot water and mix. In a small and separate bowl, mix sugar and coconut oil to make a scrub. Set aside to use after soak.

Usage

Place a large towel under foot bowl. Once all soak ingredients are mixed into the large bowl, soak feet for 15 minutes. Remove feet from water. Take a pinch of sugar scrub. Using circular motion, scrub feet and lower legs to remove any dead skin and calluses. Rinse feet in water mixture and dry. Add a small amount of coconut oil to feet and lower legs to moisturize skin.

Grilled Peaches with Rosemary and Balsamic Reduction

Simple yet versatile, these pieces of goodness can be served as an appetizer or side, or on top of your favorite frozen yogurt. Peaches are full of fiber, vitamin C, and beta-carotene. Rosemary is a rich source of antioxidants and anti-inflammatory compounds. The herb rosemary has been hailed since ancient times for its medicinal properties and is used around the world to create deep flavor in recipes.

Ingredients

3 organic peaches

4 sprigs fresh rosemary, chopped

coconut oil

1 cup balsamic vinegar

Preparation

In a medium saucepan, add balsamic vinegar and bring to a simmer over medium-high heat. Turn down heat to keep at a low simmer. It will take about 10–15 minutes to thicken and reduce. Keep a careful eye on the reduction so it doesn't burn. When it coats a spoon, it will be thick enough.

Cut each peach in half and remove pits. Brush inside of peaches lightly with coconut oil. Oil grill grates and preheat to medium-high heat.

Place peach halves with cut sides facing down. Grill for 3–4 minutes. Flip peaches over and grill for another 3–4 minutes. Remove from grill and drizzle with balsamic reduction. Sprinkle with chopped rosemary and serve.

Rosemary Oil Hair Treatment

A new take on hot-oil treatment, this aromatic oil helps to heal dry scalp and stimulate hair growth. Rosemary has been used for centuries to aid in obtaining healthy hair and scalp. It stimulates and improves circulation to the scalp, encourages hair growth, increases shine, and relieves dry, flaky scalp. Coconut oil is rich in nutrients that help stimulate hair follicles, and it helps to hydrate and seal damaged hair.

Ingredients

8–10 fresh rosemary sprigs

3/4 cup coconut oil

1 teaspoon vitamin E oil

3–4 drops peppermint essential oil (optional)

Preparation

In a bowl, crush rosemary with the back of a spoon to release oils. Pour coconut oil over the top of rosemary and stir. Transfer mixture into a small saucepan.

Cover and simmer on low heat for 25 minutes, stirring frequently. Remove from heat and let cool. Strain rosemary leaves and transfer liquid to a container with tight lid. Add vitamin E oil and peppermint essential oil. Shake well.

Usage

Cleanse hair and massage with a few tablespoons of oil mixture, then comb through hair. Place a shower cap on and allow mixture to set for at least 1 hour. Rinse hair with warm water for several minutes and style as usual.

Storage

Store remaining oil in a glass jar with tight lid. Use within two month.

Carrot-Ginger Soup with Goji Berries

This tasty soup packs a powerful antioxidant punch with carrots, goji berries, and yacon. Goji berries are a super antioxidant and are chock full of vitamins and minerals; they are an amazing anti-inflammatory. Carrots, well known for their vitamin A, which improves vision, are anti-aging, promote healthy skin, and cleanse the body. Yacon has a reputation for being one of the healthiest sweeteners due to its high content of inulin, which has a low-glycemic impact and provides healthy probiotics.

Ingredients

1 1/2 cups fresh organic carrot juice

2 tablespoons dried goji berries

2 tablespoons coconut oil

1 cup organic sweet onion, chopped

1 jalapeño pepper, minced

1 pound organic carrots, sliced into 1/4- inch rounds

1 inch chopped ginger

3 cups vegetable broth

1 tablespoon yacon syrup

1 cup water

1/2 cup light coconut milk

sea salt and pepper to taste

goji berries for garnish

organic baby arugula for garnish

Preparation

In a small bowl, mix carrot juice and goji berries. Let soak 30 minutes.

Heat coconut oil in a large pot over medium heat. Add onion and sauté for 3 minutes. Add jalapeño and cook for 1 minute. Add carrots, ginger, vegetable broth, yacon syrup, and water. Bring to boil. Cover and reduce heat to simmer, cooking for 30 minutes.

Transfer mixture to a blender. Add coconut milk and blend into a thick puree. Strain goji berries from carrot juice. Set berries aside and add juice to soup, blending until smooth. Add salt and pepper to taste.

Ladle soup into bowls and top with goji berries and baby arugula.

Carrot-Coconut Moisture Hand Mask

This hydrating hand treatment, which is loaded with amazing healing properties, revives dry hands. Packed full of vitamin A, carrots are known for their ability to stimulate cellular renewal and help to fight the signs of aging. Lemon helps to exfoliate dry skin, and coconut oil contains numerous healing properties, which improve skin's moisture and lipid content. This is a great mask for all skin types; it heals and soothes dry, aging skin.

Ingredients

1 small organic carrot

2 teaspoons coconut oil

1/2 teaspoon coconut flour

1 teaspoon organic lemon juice

Preparation

Begin by steaming the carrot until fork tender. Place steamed carrot in a mixing bowl and add coconut oil. Mash and blend well. Add coconut flour and lemon juice. Blend until a paste is formed.

Usage

Start by applying a thick layer of mask onto clean skin. Allow mask to set for 10–-15 minutes, then remove with warm water. Apply a generous amount of moisturizer or coconut oil to further hydrate skin.

Blooming Red Onion Flower

A healthier version of fried onions, these onion flowers are almost too pretty to eat and are sure to be a crowd pleaser. Onions have layers of nutrients that help protect the body. Red onions contain compounds called "flavonoids," which are the primary source of pigmentation in these vegetables. The most important of these flavonoids is quercetin, an antioxidant compound that may offer protection against cancer, heart disease, and allergies.

Ingredients

4 small organic red onions

3 tablespoons avocado oil

2 tablespoons balsamic vinegar

sea salt and pepper

Preparation

Peel onions and slice off small bottom portions of roots so they sit on flat surface. Begin by cutting onion in half, slowly starting at top and stopping about half an inch from the bottom so all pieces stay together. Cut it in half again to produce 4 segments; then cut each segment in half. You should be left with an onion cut into 8 segments, which are all joined together at the bottom.

Place onions in a bowl and drizzle with oil and vinegar. Roll them around to ensure they are well coated. Transfer to a baking dish, making sure they have enough room to spread out. Top with leftover oil and vinegar from bowl. Sprinkle with sea salt and pepper.

Cover dish with foil or parchment paper. Bake at 425 degrees F for 25–30 minutes until onions are open and slightly tender. Uncover and bake for additional 10 minutes.

Serve as a fun appetizer or side dish.

Strengthening Onion Hair Treatment

This ancient remedy leaves hair strong, protected, and healthy. Onion juice has been used since ancient times to help revive dull hair, promote growth, and prevent breakage. Onions are a rich source of sulfur, which increases the production of collagen and helps hair to grow. Coconut oil is loaded with nourishing and moisturizing properties.

Ingredients

1/4 cup organic onion juice (use white onion for blond hair)

2 tablespoons apple cider vinegar

2 tablespoons warm coconut oil

4 drops rosemary essential oil

Preparation

Combine all ingredients in a bottle and shake well.

Usage

Apply treatment to wet hair, beginning at roots. Massage in a circular motion and bring product down to ends, ensuring all hair is saturated. Place a shower cap over hair and let rest for 20 minutes. Rinse with warm water and style as usual.

Storage

Store leftovers in airtight container and keep up to 5 days.

Health Nut Banana Muffins

Bananas are the all-star of banana muffins, lending a naturally sweet taste and aroma to the treat. Bananas are a great source of carbohydrates, an essential nutrient used as fuel for mental and physical processes. Chia seeds, which are rich in omega-3, reduce food cravings, help to stay hydrated, and lower blood pressure.

Ingredients

2 small organic free-range eggs

2 ripe organic bananas

3 tablespoons raw organic honey

3 tablespoons coconut milk

1 teaspoon coconut oil

1 teaspoon pure vanilla extract

1 teaspoon baking powder

1 cup almond meal

1/2 cup plus 2 tablespoons oat flour

3 tablespoons chia seeds

optional toppings: melted cacao nibs and chopped nuts

Preparation

Preheat oven to 350 degrees F and line muffin tin with 8–10 paper liners.

In a large bowl, mix eggs and bananas until well mashed.

Add honey, coconut milk, coconut oil, pure vanilla extract, and baking powder. Stir well. Mix in almond meal, oat flour, and chia seeds, stirring until combined. Pour mixture into muffin tin.

Bake for 25–30 minutes or until toothpick or knife inserted into center comes out clean.

Remove muffins and let rest in pan for 5 minutes. If adding toppings, melt cacao nibs and drizzle over top of each muffin. Sprinkle with chopped nuts.

Moisturizing Hair Mask

This boosting banana hair mask has tons of moisturizing properties. It strengthens hair to prevent breakage and split ends, and it maintains natural hair elasticity. Bananas are incredible beauty fruits, since they are super rich in potassium; vitamins A, C, and E; and antioxidants. They contain natural oils and moisture. Coconut milk is high in vitamin E and fats that help hydrate hair.

Ingredients

1 very ripe organic banana

1 raw organic egg

2 tablespoons raw organic honey

1 tablespoon coconut milk

1/4 cup coconut oil

1/4 cup avocado oil

Preparation

Mash banana until smooth with no chunks. Set aside. Place egg, honey, and coconut milk in food processor or blender. Pulse until well combined.

While food processor or blender is still running, add oils to egg mixture until it becomes thick.

Fold egg mixture into banana and mix until a smooth paste is formed.

Usage

Start with clean, towel-dried hair. Using your hands, slather mask mixture into scalp and lengths of your hair. Cover with a shower cap and let set for at least 30 minutes.

Rinse well with warm water. Take your time to comb through hair with a light detangler or coconut oil.

Lemony Rainbow Cabbage Salad

Colorful and nutrient packed, this salad can be enjoyed anytime and reap the benefits. Purple vegetables such as cabbage contain anthocyanins, chemicals that protect the body and can decrease the spread of cancer cells. Parsley is rich in many vital vitamins, including vitamins A, B12, C, and K. Parsley keeps the immune system strong, tones bones, and heals the nervous system.

Ingredients

Salad:

About 6 cups of roughly chopped organic purple cabbage

1 organic carrot, thinly chopped

3 organic celery stalks, chopped

1 organic red pepper, thinly sliced

2 handfuls of fresh parsley, chopped finely

3–4 tablespoons of toasted sesame seeds

salt and pepper to taste

Dressing:

1/4 cup tahini

2 garlic cloves

1/2 cup fresh organic lemon juice (about 2 lemons)

1/4 cup nutritional yeast

2–4 tablespoons extra-virgin olive oil to taste

1 teaspoon kosher salt and freshly ground black pepper

3 tablespoons water

Preparation

Begin by making dressing. In a food processor, add all dressing ingredients and process until smooth. Set aside.

Bring a few cups of water to a boil. Rinse cabbage and slice in half. Chop cabbage into thin slices. Place chopped cabbage into a strainer and pour boiling water over top, then quickly rinse with cold water. This step helps to slightly soften cabbage. Roughly dry cabbage with a hand towel.

In a large bowl, mix chopped cabbage, carrot, celery, red pepper, parsley, and sesame seeds. Season with salt and pepper. Mix desired amount of dressing and toss well. Serve cold.

Lemon Nail Strengthener and Brightener

If you're like me, you talk a lot with your hands, making them a focal point for the conversation. This quick nail treatment will leave nails looking their best. Olive oil is packed with vitamins, minerals, and natural fatty acids—in particular, vitamins A and E, which help nourish and regenerate cells. Lemon helps to remove stains and fortify nails.

Ingredients

1/4 cup olive oil

2 lemons, juiced

Preparation

Mix olive oil and lemon juice.

Usage

Using a cotton swab or cotton ball, dab mixture and apply to each nail. Massage into nails and cuticles. Allow serum to penetrate and do not remove. Use daily to hydrate, brighten, and nourish nails.

Storage

Store in a glass jar with tight lid. Make sure to dip clean cotton swab or ball into the solution to ensure no contamination. Store for up to 1 month.

Beet Detox Juice

This simple yet effective juice helps to cleanse the liver and boost your body's natural detox mechanisms. Beets are a rich source of phytonutrients like betanin that have strong anti-inflammatory and antioxidant properties, coupled with a stimulating effect on the various detoxification pathways of the body, especially the liver. Carrots are some of the best known sources of vitamin A, beta-carotene, and alpha-carotene; these protect the body from free radical damage.

Ingredients

1 small organic beet

2 organic carrots

2 organic apples

1 handful organic kale

1/2-inch organic ginger root, peeled

1/2 organic lemon, peeled

Preparation

Juice all ingredients and mix well. Serve and enjoy. Refrigerate any leftovers. It is best used within 2 days.

Beet Lip Stain

Lip stains are the perfect way to give your puckers just a touch of color. This organic and natural lip stain is chemical free and sure to please. Beets give the lip stain a beautiful tint and are loaded with vitamins and minerals to help keep lips kissable and looking their best.

Ingredients

3 tablespoons non-GMO vegetable glycerin

1 tablespoon grated beeswax

1/2 medium-sized beet, chopped

Preparation

Fill a double boiler with water. Heat water to boil, then reduce to a gentle rolling bubble. Place glycerin, beeswax, and chopped beets into a glass measuring cup and heat for 25 minutes. Beets should be soft, and glycerin should have a bright-red shade. Place liquid and beets through a sieve and pour liquid into desired container, ensuring no bits come through. Let cool to solidify. Use on lips or cheeks as a nice blush.

Printed in the United States
By Bookmasters